COOL CARS

LAMBORGHINI AVENTADOR

BY KAITLYN DULING

EPIC

BELLWETHER MEDIA ››› MINNEAPOLIS, MN

EPIC BOOKS are no ordinary books. They burst with intense action, high-speed heroics, and shadows of the unknown. Are you ready for an Epic adventure?

This edition first published in 2024 by Bellwether Media, Inc.

No part of this publication may be reproduced in whole or in part without written permission of the publisher. For information regarding permission, write to Bellwether Media, Inc., Attention: Permissions Department, 6012 Blue Circle Drive, Minnetonka, MN 55343.

Library of Congress Cataloging-in-Publication Data

Names: Duling, Kaitlyn, author.
Title: Lamborghini Aventador / by Kaitlyn Duling.
Description: Minneapolis, MN : Bellwether Media, 2024. | Series: Cool cars. | Includes bibliographical references and index. | Audience: Ages 7-12 | Audience: Grades 2-3 | Summary: "Engaging images accompany information about the Lamborghini Aventador. The combination of high-interest subject matter and light text is intended for students in grades 2 through 7"--Provided by publisher.
Identifiers: LCCN 2023001645 (print) | LCCN 2023001646 (ebook) | ISBN 9798886874990 (library binding) | ISBN 9798886876871 (ebook)
Subjects: LCSH: Lamborghini automobile--Juvenile literature. | Sports cars--Juvenile literature. | CYAC: Vehicles.
Classification: LCC TL215.L33 D85 2024 (print) | LCC TL215.L33 (ebook) | DDC 629.222/2--dc23/eng/20230113
LC record available at https://lccn.loc.gov/2023001645
LC ebook record available at https://lccn.loc.gov/2023001646

Text copyright © 2024 by Bellwether Media, Inc. EPIC and associated logos are trademarks and/or registered trademarks of Bellwether Media, Inc.

Editor: Rachael Barnes   Designer: Jeffrey Kollock

Printed in the United States of America, North Mankato, MN.

TABLE OF CONTENTS

SPEED AND STYLE	4
ALL ABOUT THE AVENTADOR	6
PARTS OF THE AVENTADOR	12
THE AVENTADOR'S FUTURE	20
GLOSSARY	22
TO LEARN MORE	23
INDEX	24

SPEED AND STYLE

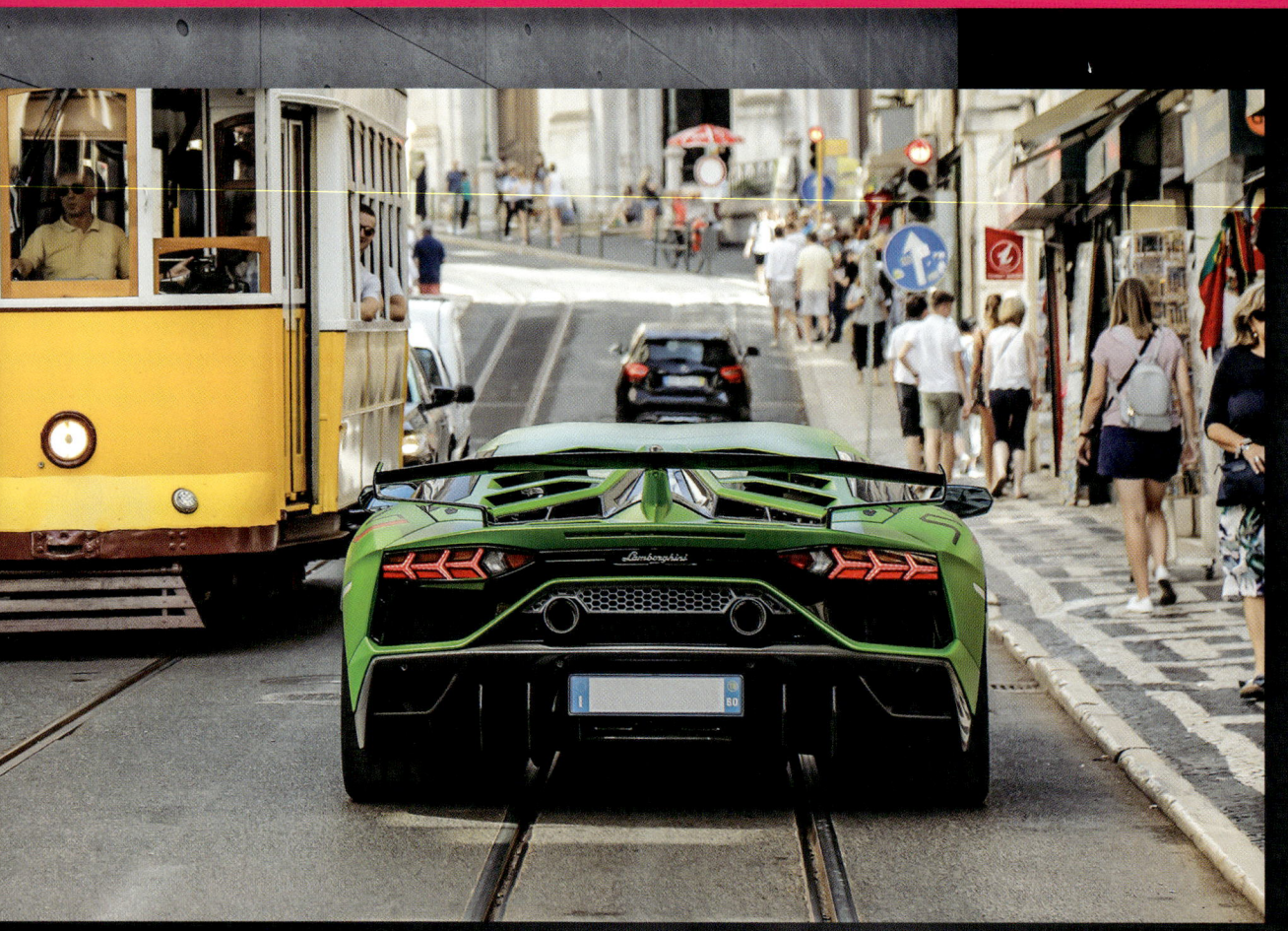

A Lamborghini Aventador is stopped at a red light. It is a work of art.

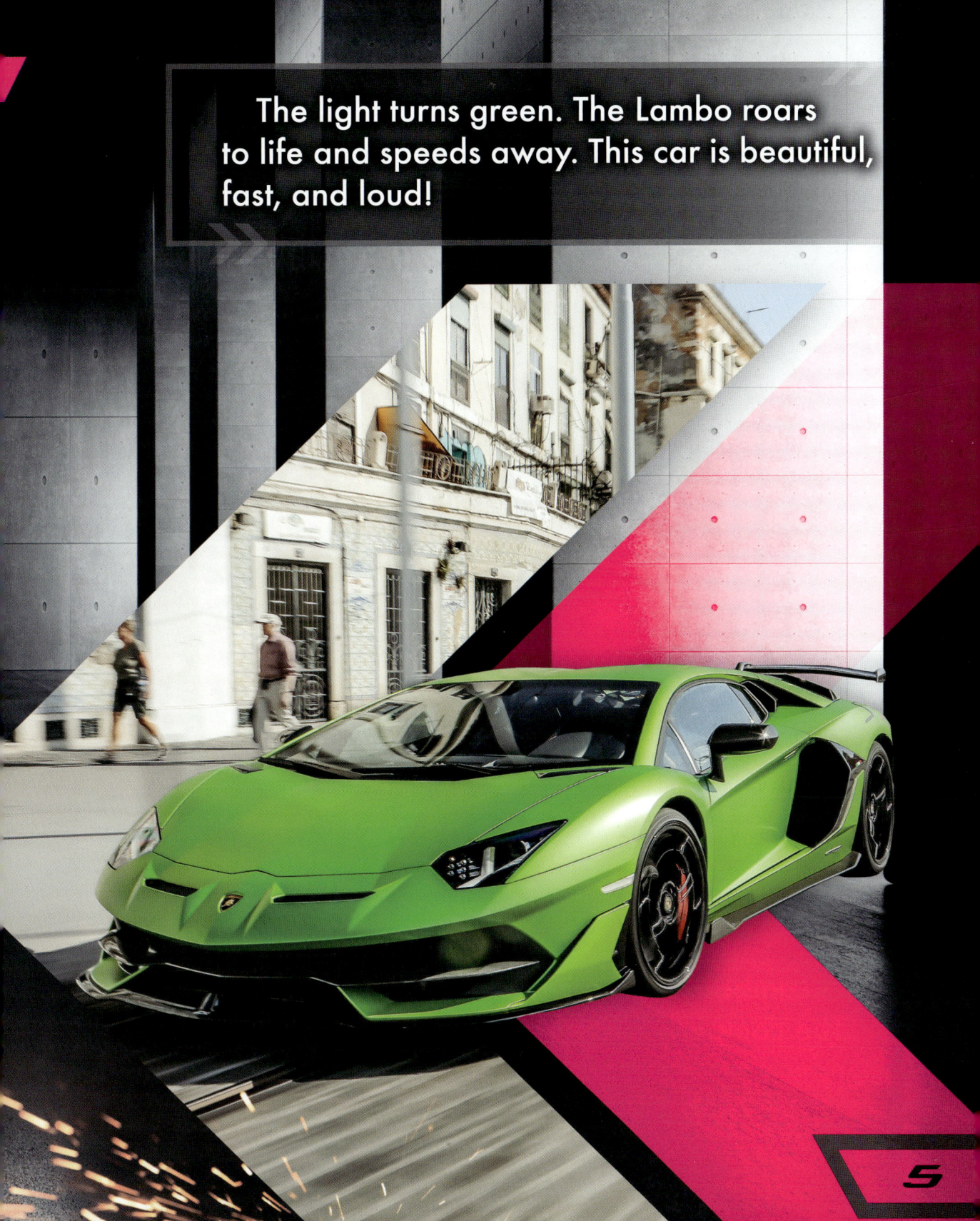

The light turns green. The Lambo roars to life and speeds away. This car is beautiful, fast, and loud!

ALL ABOUT THE AVENTADOR »

1963 350 GTV

Lamborghini started in Italy in 1963. The company's first car was the 350 GTV.

Today, the company is known for fast **luxury** sports cars. The Huracán and Centenario are well-known **models**.

CENTENARIO

📍 WHERE IS IT MADE?

EUROPE

SANT'AGATA BOLOGNESE, ITALY

The Aventador was first sold in 2011. It became the company's **flagship**. Each car was built by hand in Italy. Thousands were sold. Owners could choose the colors, tires, and more.

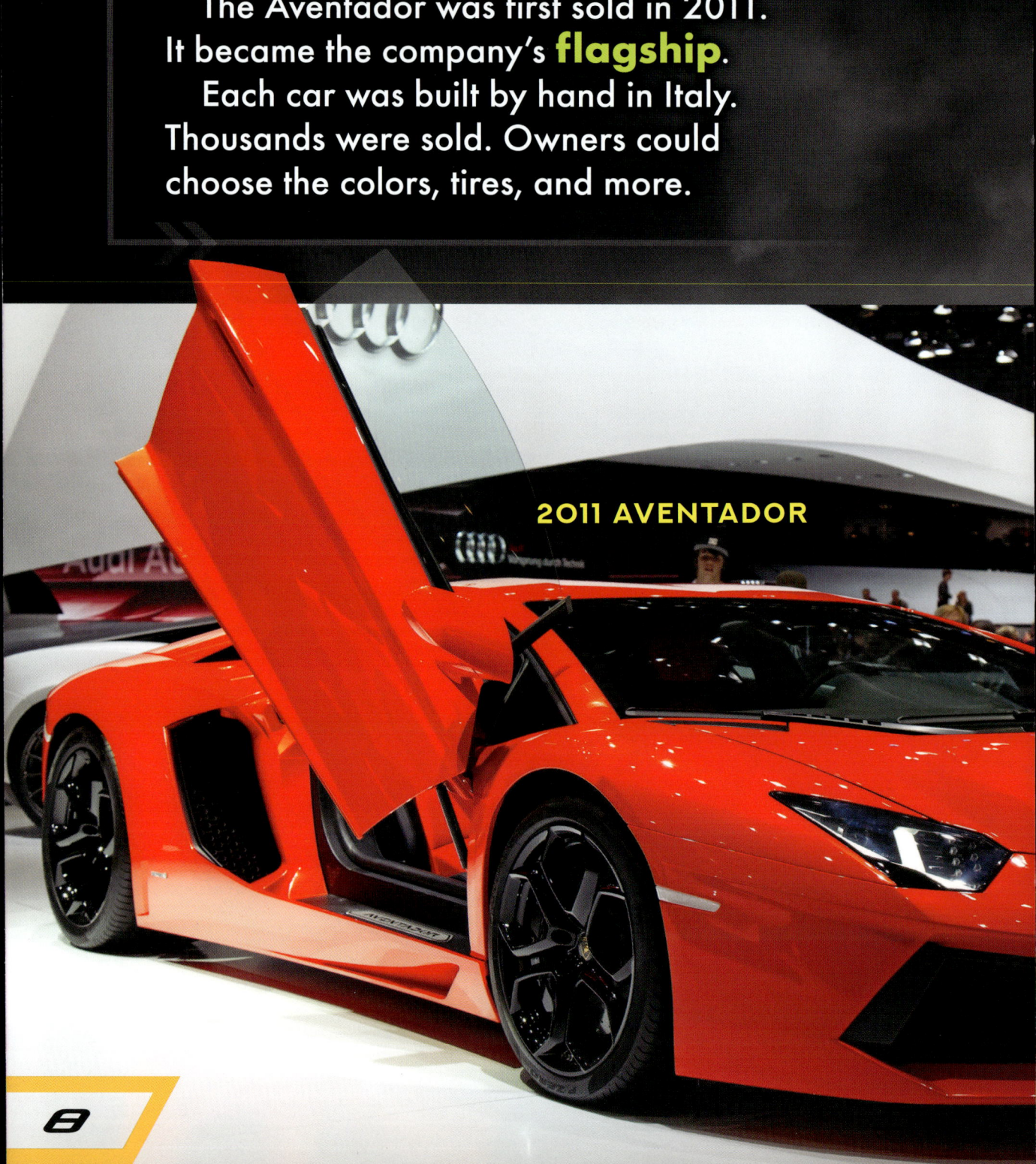

2011 AVENTADOR

AVENTADOR BASICS

LP 780-4 ULTIMAE

YEAR FIRST MADE 2011

COST started at $501,953 in 2022

HOW MANY MADE 600 in 2022

FEATURES

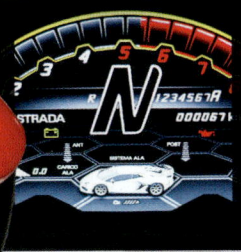

automated manual transmission

carbon fiber body

air intakes

When it is on the track, the Aventador records lap times. It has three different drive modes.

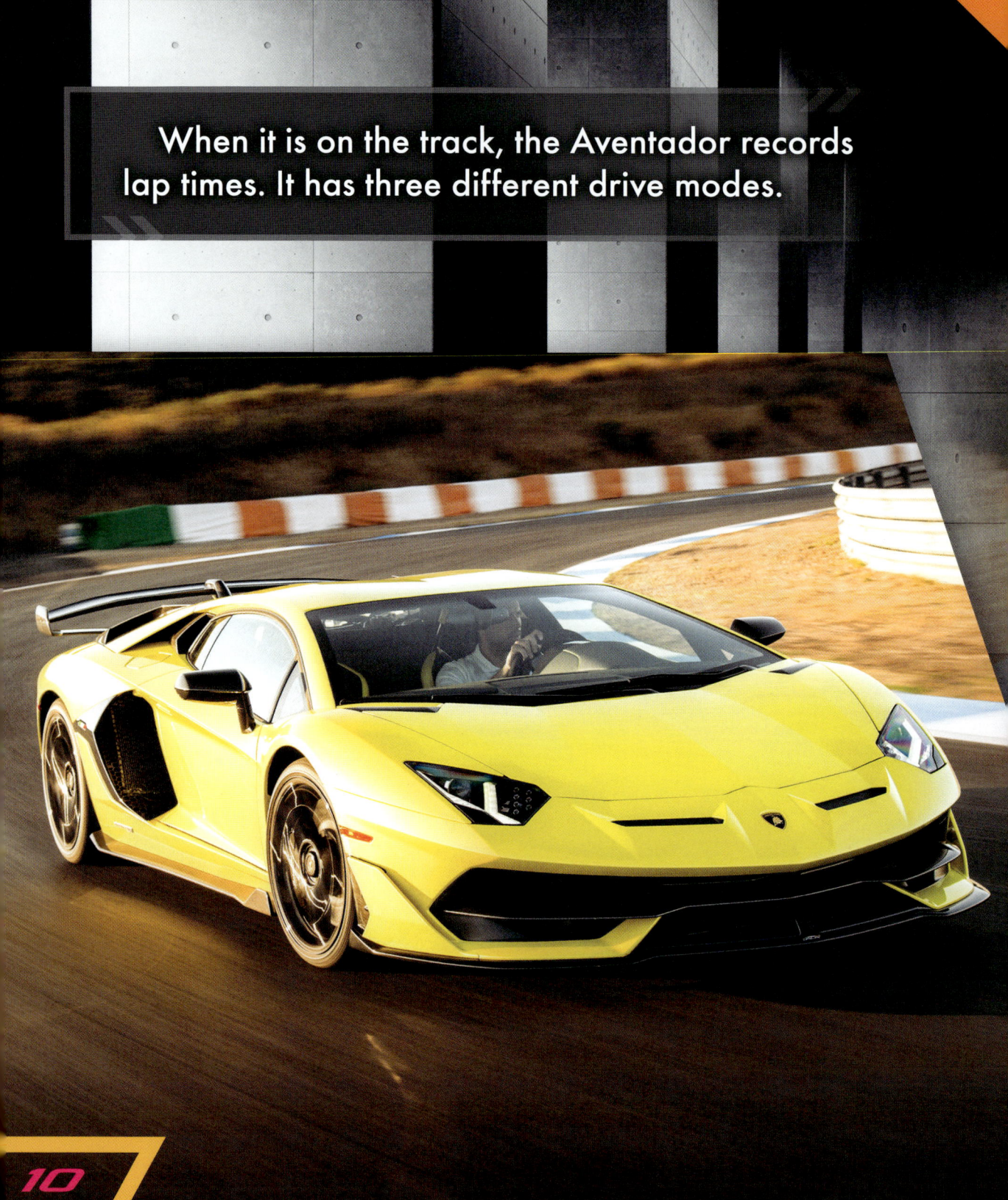

FIGHTING WORDS

Many Lamborghinis are named after famous fighting bulls. Aventador was an award-winning bull that fought in Spain in 1993.

It is also safe to drive on the highway. The Aventador is quick to start on tracks and roads!

PARTS OF THE AVENTADOR

The Aventador has a powerful and loud **V12 engine**. It can produce up to 769 **horsepower**! Its **automated manual transmission** sends power to all four wheels.

 ENGINE SPECS

V12 ENGINE

TOP SPEED — 221 miles (355 kilometers) per hour

0-62 TIME — 2.8 seconds

HORSEPOWER — 769 hp

The Aventador is built for speed. Its body is made with **carbon fiber**.

CARBON FIBER

SIZE CHART

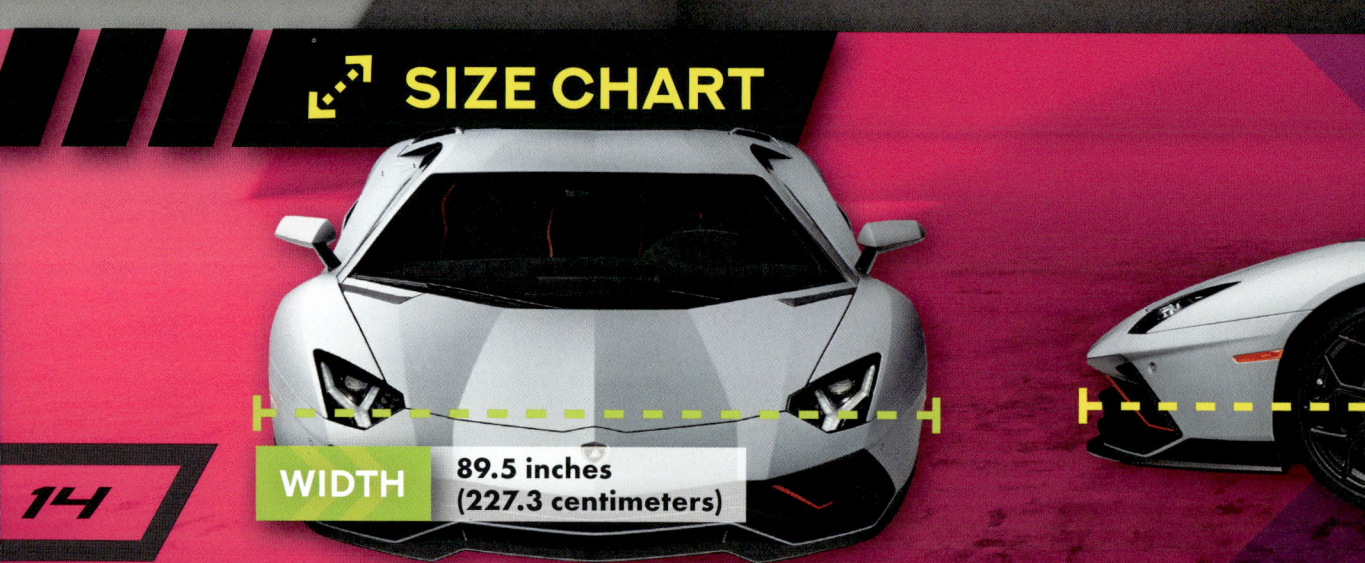

WIDTH 89.5 inches (227.3 centimeters)

The low, wide shape is **aerodynamic**. The car's pointed nose pushes air over the body. **Air intakes** move air into the engine.

‹‹‹ AIR INTAKE

HEIGHT 44.7 inches (113.6 centimeters)

LENGTH 191.7 inches (486.8 centimeters)

««« SCISSOR DOORS »»»

FLYING HIGH
The Aventador's design was inspired by the F-35 Lightning, a famous fighter jet.

Aventador owners could choose **scissor doors** that swing up to open. They could also pick the body color of the car from hundreds of options.

Inside, two seats sit low to the ground. They came in many colors, too.

The Aventador was sold in several **trims**. Aventador Roadsters have a removable roof. The Aventador J has no roof or windows.

AVENTADOR S ROADSTER

AS SEEN IN

The Aventador has appeared in many action movies. It can be seen in *Transformers: Age of Extinction*, *The Dark Knight Rises*, and *Furious 7*.

AVENTADOR LP 780-4 ULTIMAE

The final trim, the LP 780-4 Ultimae, has the most powerful V12 engine in Lamborghini history.

THE AVENTADOR'S FUTURE »

Lamborghini stopped making the Aventador in 2022. The next flagship car will be a plug-in **hybrid**. The company will make **electric** models, too. Future Lambos will be beautiful, fast, and better for the planet!

GLOSSARY

aerodynamic—able to move through air easily

air intakes—openings on a car that allow air to reach its engine

automated manual transmission—a car part that has a clutch and changes gears automatically; a clutch is the part of a car that moves power from the engine to the wheels.

carbon fiber—a strong, lightweight material used to strengthen things

electric—able to run using electricity instead of gasoline

flagship—a car company's best and most important model

horsepower—a measurement of the power of an engine or motor

hybrid—a car that uses both a gasoline engine and an electric motor for power

luxury—having a high level of comfort

models—specific kinds of cars

scissor doors—doors that open upwards, rather than outwards

trims—models of a car with specific sets of features and equipment

V12 engine—an engine with 12 cylinders arranged in the shape of a "V"

TO LEARN MORE

AT THE LIBRARY

Adamson, Thomas K. *Lamborghini Huracán Evo*. Minneapolis, Minn.: Bellwether Media, 2023.

Colby, Jennifer. *Lamborghini*. Ann Arbor, Mich.: Cherry Lake Publishing, 2023.

Garstecki, Julia. *Lamborghini Aventador*. Mankato, Minn.: Black Rabbit Books, 2020.

ON THE WEB

Factsurfer.com gives you a safe, fun way to find more information.

1. Go to www.factsurfer.com.

2. Enter "Lamborghini Aventador" into the search box and click 🔍.

3. Select your book cover to see a list of related content.

INDEX

aerodynamic, 15
air intakes, 15
automated manual transmission, 12
basics, 9
body, 14, 15, 16
colors, 8, 16, 17
drive modes, 10
electric, 20
engine, 12, 15, 19
engine specs, 12
F-35 Lightning, 16
flagship, 8, 20
future, 20
history, 6, 8, 19, 20
horsepower, 12
hybrid, 20
Italy, 6, 7, 8

Lamborghini (company), 6, 7, 8, 19, 20
models, 6, 7, 20
movies, 19
name, 11
roads, 11
roof, 18
scissor doors, 16
seats, 17
size chart, 14–15
tires, 8
track, 10, 11
trims, 18, 19
wheels, 12
windows, 18

The images in this book are reproduced through the courtesy of: Lamborghini, front cover, pp. 3, 4, 5, 6, 7, 9 (air intakes), 10, 11, 12-13, 14 (width), 15, 14-15 (length), 16-17, 18, 19, 20, 21; Fedor Selivanov, pp. 8-9; ThatCarPhotographer, p. 9 (body); classic topcar, p. 9 (transmission); Tuner tom, p. 12 (engine); Brandon Woyshnis, p. 14; Composite_Carbonman, p. 14 (carbon fiber); Car_Photographer, p. 16.